AF326750

-With thanks to-

Claudia, you brought my vision to life with your incredible illustrations!

My husband, I could not have created this book without your support and creative eye. I am the best version of myself with you.

My son, I wrote this while I was pregnant with you! You gave me the creative spark, time and patience to sit and write. Now we can read this together!

My Dad, you inspired me with your terrible jokes, especially the one about "burping from the other end"- there will always be a piece of my childhood in this book.

My Mum, you nurtured my vocabulary from a young age, even though English was your second language. You did not want me to struggle at school the way you did, and I am so grateful for my education thanks to you.

My speech pathology clients and co-workers, thank you for reigniting my passion for telling stories, teaching and laughing along the way.

To all my friends and family, thank you for sharing this journey with me.

See you "at the other end"

-Shirley Hassarati-

A Burp from the Other End

Written by Shirley Hassarati
Illustrated by Claudia Stafrace

Copyright © 2025 Shirley Hassarati

All rights reserved. No part of this book may be reproduced in any manner whatsoever without prior written permission of the publisher.

First Printing, 2025

Published by Shirley Hassarati - M&S Hassarati PTY LTD
https://www.instagram.com/shirleys.stories/

ISBN 978-1-7643611-0-1

A BURP from the other end

buuuu

uurrrrrrrrpppp

Sorry for my rudeness
I know it was not smart
But if it came out the other end...

Could it have been a dart?
A dart is good for throwing
Bullseye! You win!

But the thing that
I am thinking of
will usually
pass as wind...

Sorry for my rudeness
I know it was not smart
But if it came out the other end...

Could it have been a cart?
Carts are good for shopping
And carrying the load

But the thing
that I am
thinking of
usually
explodes!

Sorry for my rudeness
I know it was not smart
But if it came out the other end...

Could it have been a tart?
I love tarts filled with lemons
I can eat them in seconds

They go
straight
to my belly
but they are
not so smelly...

Sorry for my rudeness
I know it was not smart
But if it came out the other end...

Could it have been a chart?
Charts are great for counting
They can be square or round

But the thing that
I am thinking of
Simply cannot
be found

Sorry for my rudeness
I know it was not smart
But if it came out the
other end

it WOULD have been a...

FART
Oops...
Excuse me!

haha
burrrpp
pffffft
pop
toot
eww

BLANKS LEVELS OF QUESTIONING

Level 1

1. Point to one of the darts and say "Find one like this"
2. Point to a familiar grocery item and ask "What is this?"
3. Point to the lemon and ask "What colour is this?"
4. Ask the child to show you something e.g. "Show me the cat"

Level 2

1. "Tell me about this dart" allow them to describe the features.
2. Point to a familiar grocery item and ask "What is this used for?"
3. Point to a baking tool and say "Tell me about this thing."
4. Point to the charts and ask "How are these different?"

Ask 1 question after making at least 4 comments to have a balanced interaction.

Wait for a response before repeating or rephrasing.

1. Ask the child to "Name something you can aim, that is not a dart"
2. Point to the grocery items and say "Find the ones that are not liquids"
3. Ask the child to "Find the things that are not hot"
4. Point to the charts and ask "How are these the same?"

Level 3

1. Ask "What will happen if the dart hits this red circle?"
2. Point to the groceries and ask "What could we use to make breakfast?"
3. Ask "Why should we measure ingredients when we bake?"
4. Point to the pink character and ask "How can we tell that this one likes counting?"

Level 4

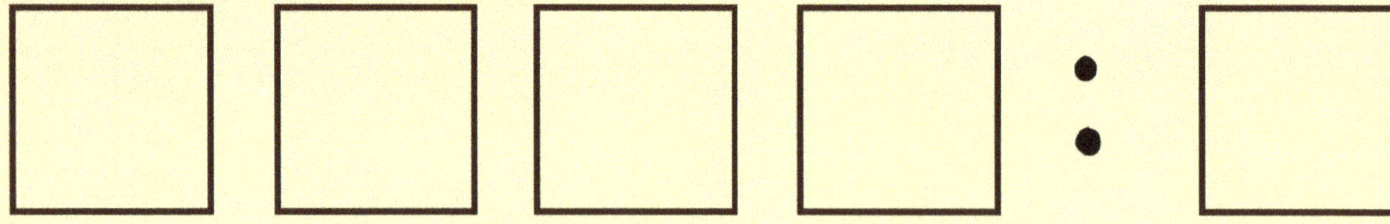

I SPY

with my little eye something beginning with....

www.ingramcontent.com/pod-product-compliance
Lightning Source LLC
Chambersburg PA
CBHW040907070726
47599CB00038B/2339
9781764361101